This Book
Belongs To

A BIBLE VERSE COLORING BOOK

Inspirational Christian Coloring Books for Adults

OANCEA CAMELIA

Behold,
I am with you
always,
even to the end
of the AGE.
MATTHEW 28:20

Fear not, for I am with thee; be not dismayed, for I am thy GOD.

Submit yourselves, then, to God.
Resist the devil, and he will flee from you.
James 4:7

You make known to me the path of life;
you will fill me with joy in your presence,
with eternal pleasures at your right hand.
Psalm 16:11

I write these things to you who believe in the name
of the Son of God so that you may know
that you have eternal life.
John 5:13

For I take no pleasure in the death of anyone, declares the Sovereign LORD. Repent and live!
Ezekiel 18:32

Do not think that I have come
to send peace upon the earth:
I have not come to send peace,
but a sword.
Matthew 10:34

The Lord is my helper.
Hebrews 13:6

For it is by grace you have been saved, through faith—and this is not from yourselves, it is the gift of God.
Ephesians 2:8

Do not be misled:
"Bad company corrupts good character."
Corinthians 15:33

This is the confidence we have in approaching God:
that if we ask anything according to his will, he hears us.
John 5:14

Let the peace of Christ rule in your hearts, since as members of one body you were called to peace. And be thankful.
Colossians 3:15

MAKE EVERY EFFORT TO LIVE IN PEACE WITH EVERYONE AND TO BE HOLY WITHOUT HOLINESS NO ONE WILL SEE THE LORD.
Hebrews 12:14

"Yet when planted,
it grows and becomes
the largest
of all garden plants,
with such big branches
that the birds can perch
in its shade."
Mark 4:32

I warn everyone who hears the words
of the prophecy of this scroll:
If anyone adds anything to them,
God will add to that person the plagues
described in this scroll.

Revelation 22:18

WE LOVE HIM
BECAUSE
HE FIRST
LOVED US.
John 4:19

This hope we have as an anchor of the soul,
a hope both sure and steadfast
and entering into that which is within the veil.
Hebrews 6:19

Consider the lilies of the field,
how they grow; they toil not,
neither do they spin:
Matthew 6:28

He has made everything beautiful in its time.
Ecclesiastes 3:11

Be strong
and courageous.
Do not be afraid,
neither be
dismayed.

I am the vine;
you are the branches.
If you remain in me and I in you,
you will bear much fruit;
apart from me
you can do nothing.
John 15:5

Let your beauty
be not just the outward
adorning of braiding the hair,
and of wearing jewels of gold,
or of putting on fine clothing.

Peter 3:3

Cast your burden upon the LORD, and He will sustain you.
Psalm 55:22

Ye are the light of the world.
Matthew 5:14

She considereth a field,
and buyeth it;
With the fruit of her hands
she planteth a vineyard.
Proverbs 31:16

He who testifies to these things says,
"Yes, I am coming soon." Amen. Come, Lord Jesus.
Revelation 22:20

EVEN THOUGH I WALK
THROUGH THE VALLEY
OF THE SHADOW OF DEATH,
I WILL FEAR NO EVIL,
FOR YOU ARE WITH ME.
PSALM 23: 4

Love thy neighbor as thyself.
Mark 12:31

In all thy ways acknowledge him,
and he shall direct thy paths.
Proverbs 3:6

In nothing be anxious;
but in everything by prayer
and supplication
with thanksgiving
let your requests be made
known unto God.
And the peace of God,
which passeth all understanding,
shall guard your hearts and
your thoughts in Christ Jesus.
Philippians 4:6-7

O Lord, have mercy on us: for we have waited for thee:
be thou our strength in the morning,
and our salvation in the time of trouble.
Isaiah 33:2

For every animal
of the forest is mine,
and the livestock
on a thousand hills.
Psalm 50:10

Be still,
and know that I am God.
Psalm 46:10

The grass withers,
the flower fades;
but the word of our God
stands forever.
Isaiah 40:8

The Lord bless thee,
and keep thee:
The Lord make his face
to shine upon thee,
and be gracious unto thee:
The Lord lift up
his countenance upon thee,
and give thee peace.
Numbers 6: 24-26

For everything there is a season,
and a time for every purpose under heaven:
a time to be born, and a time to die;
a time to plant, and a time to pluck up that which is planted;
a time to kill, and a time to heal;
a time to break down, and a time to build up;
a time to weep, and a time to laugh;
a time to mourn, and a time to dance;
a time to cast away stones, and a time to gather stones together;
a time to embrace, and a time to refrain from embracing;
a time to seek, and a time to lose;
a time to keep, and a time to cast away;
a time to tear, and a time to sew;
a time to keep silence, and a time to speak;
a time to love, and a time to hate;
a time for war, and a time for peace.

Elijah said to Elisha, "Stay here;
the LORD has sent me to Bethel.
"But Elisha said,
"As surely as the LORD
lives and as you live,
I will not leave you."
So they went down to Bethel.
Kings 2:2

For thou art my lamp, O Lord:
and the Lord will lighten my darkness.
2 Samuel 22:29

Be not thou far from me,

O Lord: O my strength,

hasten to help me.

Psalm 22:19

Oh that I had wings like a dove!
for then would I fly away,
and be at rest.
Psalm 55:6

He
will be
LIKE A TREE
planted by
THE STREAMS
of water,
THAT PRODUCES
its fruit in its season.
Psalm 1:3

When Job's three friends, Eliphaz the Temanite,
Bildad the Shuhite and Zophar the Naamathite,
heard about all the troubles that had come upon him,
they set out from their homes and met together
by agreement to go and sympathize with him and comfort him.

Behold,
I am with you
always, even
to the end
of the age.
Matthew 28:20

WE LOVE HIM
BECAUSE
HE FIRST
LOVED US.
John 4:19

Therefore will we not fear
though the earth be removed,
and though the mountains
be carried into the heart of the seas.
Psalm 46:2

Be strong, and let your heart
take courage,
all you who hope
in the LORD.
PSALM 31:24

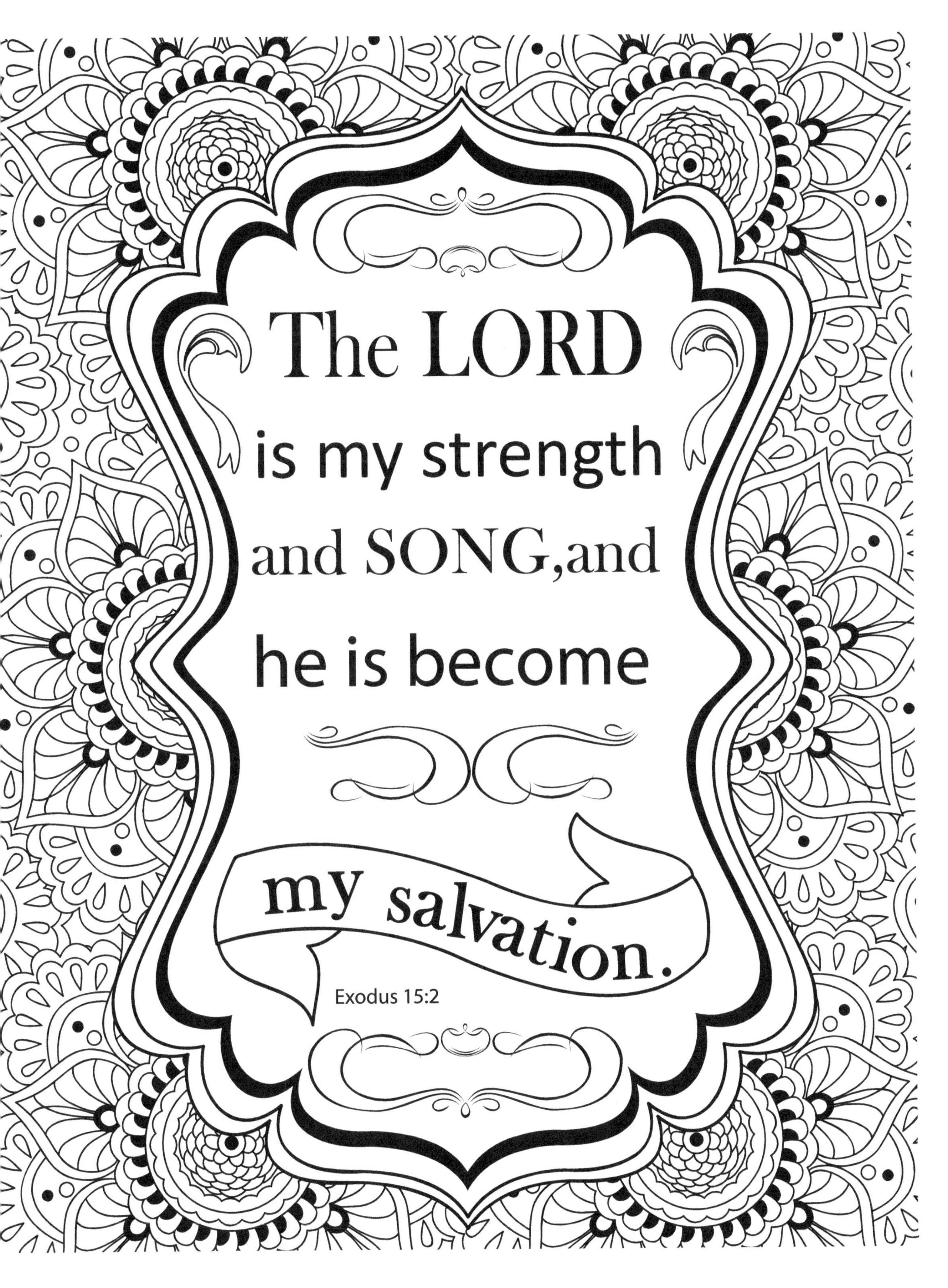

The LORD
is my strength
and SONG,and
he is become
my salvation.
Exodus 15:2

As the deer pants for the water brooks,
so my soul pants after you, God.
Psalm 42:1

When
you pass
through the waters,
I will be with you;
and through the rivers,
they will not
overflow
you.

Isaiah 43:2

"You ARE my HIDING place and my SHIELD"
PSALM 119:114